Congressional
Research
Service ─────────────────────────────────

Introduction to the Federal Budget Process

Bill Heniff Jr., Coordinator
Analyst on Congress and the Legislative Process

Megan Suzanne Lynch
Analyst on Congress and the Legislative Process

Jessica Tollestrup
Analyst on Congress and the Legislative Process

December 3, 2012

Congressional Research Service

7-5700

www.crs.gov

98-721

CRS Report for Congress ─────────────────────────────

Prepared for Members and Committees of Congress

Summary

Budgeting for the federal government is an enormously complex process. It entails dozens of subprocesses, countless rules and procedures, the efforts of tens of thousands of staff persons in the executive and legislative branches, millions of work hours each year, and the active participation of the President and congressional leaders, as well as other members of Congress and executive officials.

The enforcement of budgetary decisions involves a complex web of procedures that encompasses both congressional and executive actions. In the last four decades or so, these procedures have been rooted principally in two statutes—the Congressional Budget Act of 1974 and the Balanced Budget and Emergency Deficit Control Act of 1985. The 1974 act established a congressional budget process in which budget policies are enforced by Congress during the consideration of individual measures. The 1985 act embodies additional statutory enforcement procedures, substantially modified in 1990 and 1997, that have been used by the executive to enforce budget policies after the end of a congressional session. The 1997 iteration of these enforcement procedures were set aside in the latter years of their existence and effectively expired toward the end of the 107th Congress. Efforts to renew them in the 108th through 110th Congresses were not successful. In the 111th Congress, the pay-as-you-go procedures affecting direct spending and revenue legislation were restored in a modified version by the Statutory Pay-As-You-Go Act of 2010. More recently, in the 112th Congress, statutory limits on discretionary spending and a new automatic process to reduce spending were established by the Budget Control Act of 2011.

The President's budget is required by law to be submitted to Congress early in the legislative session. While the budget is only a request to Congress, the power to formulate and submit the budget is a vital tool in the President's direction of the executive branch and of national policy. The President's proposals often influence congressional revenue and spending decisions, though the extent of the influence varies from year to year and depends more on political and fiscal conditions than on the legal status of the budget.

The Congressional Budget Act of 1974 establishes the congressional budget process as the means by which Congress coordinates the various budget-related actions (such as the consideration of appropriations and revenue measures) taken by it during the course of the year. The process is centered on an annual concurrent resolution on the budget that sets aggregate budget policies and functional spending priorities for at least the next five fiscal years. Because a concurrent resolution is not a law—it cannot be signed or vetoed by the President—the budget resolution does not have statutory effect; no money can be raised or spent pursuant to it. Revenue and spending amounts set in the budget resolution establish the basis for the enforcement of congressional budget policies through points of order.

Congress implements budget resolution policies through action on individual revenue and debt-limit measures, annual appropriations acts, and direct spending legislation. In some years, Congress considers reconciliation legislation pursuant to reconciliation instructions in the budget resolution. Reconciliation legislation is used mainly to bring existing revenue and direct spending laws into conformity with budget resolution policies. Initially, reconciliation was a major tool for deficit reduction; in later years, reconciliation was used mainly to reduce revenues.

Contents

The Evolution of Federal Budgeting 1

Basic Concepts of Federal Budgeting 2

Budget Authority and Outlays 2
Scope of the Budget 3

Deficit Reduction and the Rules of Congressional Budgeting 4

Budgeting for Discretionary and Direct Spending 6

Budgeting for Direct and Guaranteed Loans 9

The Budget Cycle 9

The Presidential Budget Process 9

Formulation and Content of the President's Budget 10
Executive Interaction with Congress 11

The Congressional Budget Process 11

Formulation and Content of the Budget Resolution 12
Budget Resolution Enforcement 14
Budget Resolution Aggregates 14
Allocations of Spending to Committees 14
Scoring and Cost Estimates 15
Points of Order 15

The Sequestration Process 16

Spending Legislation 19

Authorizing Measures 20
The Annual Appropriations Process 20

Revenue Legislation 22

Debt-Limit Legislation 23

Reconciliation Legislation 24

Reconciliation Directives 24
Development and Consideration of Reconciliation Measures 25

House and Senate Earmark Disclosure Rules 26

House of Representatives 26
The Senate 27

Impoundment and Line-Item Veto 28

Impoundment 28
Rescissions 28
Deferrals 28
Line-Item Veto 29

Tables

Table 1. Congressional Budget Process Timetable 12

Contacts

Author Contact Information.. 30

Acknowledgments 30

The Evolution of Federal Budgeting

The "power of the purse" is a legislative power. The Constitution lists the power to lay and collect taxes and the power to borrow as powers of Congress; further, it provides that funds may be drawn from the Treasury only pursuant to appropriations made by law. The Constitution does not state how these legislative powers are to be exercised, nor does it expressly provide for the President to have a role in the management of the nation's finances.

During the nation's early years, the House and Senate devised procedures for the enactment of spending and revenue legislation. As these procedures evolved during the 19th century and the first decades of the 20th century, they led to highly fragmented legislative actions. In the course of each session, Congress passed many separate appropriations bills and other measures affecting the financial condition of the federal government. Neither the Constitution nor the procedures adopted by the House and Senate provided for a budget system—that is, for a coordinated set of actions covering all federal spending and revenues. As long as the federal government was small and its spending and revenues were stable, such a budget system was not considered necessary.

Early in the 20th century, the incessant rise in federal spending and the recurrence of deficits (spending exceeded revenues in half of the 20 years preceding FY1920) led Congress to seek a more coordinated means of making financial decisions. The key legislation was the Budget and Accounting Act of 1921, which established the executive budget process.

The 1921 act did not directly alter the procedures by which Congress makes revenue and spending decisions. The main impact was in the executive branch. The President was required to submit his budget recommendations to Congress each year, and the Bureau of the Budget—renamed the Office of Management and Budget (OMB) in 1970—was created to assist him in carrying out his budgetary responsibilities. Congress, it was expected, would be able to coordinate its revenue and spending decisions if it received comprehensive budget recommendations from the President. In line with this expectation, the House and Senate changed their rules to consolidate the jurisdiction of the Appropriations Committees over spending. The 1921 act also established the General Accounting Office (GAO), headed by the Comptroller General, and made it the principal auditing arm of the federal government. (The GAO recently was renamed the Government Accountability Office.) The 1921 act, as amended, remains the statutory basis for the presidential budget system.

After World War II, the belief that the presidential budget sufficed to maintain fiscal control gave way to the view that Congress needed its own budget process. Some members of Congress feared that dependence on the executive budget had bolstered the President's fiscal powers at the expense of Congress's; others felt that as long as its financial decisions were fragmented, Congress could not effectively control expenditures.

The Congressional Budget and Impoundment Control Act of 1974 established a congressional budget process centered on a concurrent resolution on the budget, scheduled for adoption prior to legislative consideration of revenue or spending bills. The congressional budget process initiated in the 1970s did not replace the preexisting revenue and spending processes. Instead, it provided an overall legislative framework within which the many separate measures affecting the budget would be considered. The central purpose of the budget process established by the 1974 act is to coordinate the various revenue and spending decisions which are made in separate revenue, appropriations, and other budgetary measures. To assist Congress in making budget decisions, the

1974 act established the Congressional Budget Office (CBO) and directed it to provide data on and analyses of the federal budget.

During the years that the congressional budget process has been in operation, its procedures have been adapted by Congress to changing circumstances. Following a decade of experience with the 1974 Congressional Budget Act, Congress made further changes in the budget process by enacting the Balanced Budget and Emergency Deficit Control Act of 1985 (also known as the Gramm-Rudman-Hollings Act), the Budget Enforcement Act of 1990 (BEA), the Line Item Veto Act in 1996, the Budget Enforcement Act of 1997, the Statutory Pay-As-You-Go Act of 2010, and the Budget Control Act of 2011, among other laws.

The 1985 act prescribed declining deficit targets intended to achieve balance in FY1991; the targets were enforced by sequestration, a process involving automatic, across-the-board cuts in nonexempt spending programs if the targets were expected to be exceeded. The 1990 act replaced the deficit targets with caps on discretionary spending and a pay-as-you-go (PAYGO) requirement for revenue and direct spending legislation; sequestration was retained as the means of enforcing the two new mechanisms. The 1996 act authorized the President to cancel discretionary spending in appropriation acts, as well as new direct spending and limited tax benefits in other legislation, subject to expedited legislative procedures by which Congress could overturn the cancellations. (The Supreme Court struck down the Line Item Veto Act in June 1998 as unconstitutional.) The 1997 act extended the BEA procedures for several more years. Without a consensus on extending the control mechanisms under the BEA, however, they expired at the end of FY2002. The Statutory Pay-As-You-Go Act of 2010 restored a modified version of the PAYGO requirement for direct spending and revenue legislation. More recently, as part of an agreement to increase the statutory limit on the public debt, the Budget Control Act of 2011 restored statutory limits on discretionary spending for each fiscal year through FY2021 and established an automatic process to reduce spending if subsequent legislation reducing the deficit by at least $1.2 trillion was not enacted, with spending reductions beginning in January 2013.

Basic Concepts of Federal Budgeting

The federal budget is a compilation of numbers about the revenues, spending, and borrowing and debt of the government. Revenues come largely from taxes, but stem from other sources as well (such as duties, fines, licenses, and gifts). Spending involves such concepts as budget authority, obligations, outlays, and offsetting collections. The numbers are computed according to rules and conventions that have accumulated over the years; they do not always conform to the way revenues and spending are accounted for in other processes.

Budget Authority and Outlays

When Congress appropriates money, it provides *budget authority*, that is, authority to enter into obligations. Budget authority also may be provided in legislation that does not go through the appropriations process (*direct spending* legislation). The key congressional spending decisions relate to the obligations that agencies are authorized to incur during a fiscal year, not to the outlays made during the year. (*Obligations* occur when agencies enter into contracts, submit purchase orders, employ personnel, and so forth; *outlays* occur when obligations are liquidated, primarily through the issuance of checks, electronic fund transfers, or the disbursement of cash.)

The provision of budget authority is the key point at which Congress exercises control over federal spending, although the outlay level often receives greater public attention because of its bearing on the deficit. Congress does not directly control outlays; each year's outlays derive in part from new budget authority and in part from "carryover" budget authority provided in prior years. For example, President Barack Obama's initial budget submission for FY2013 estimated that outlays would total $3,803 billion for that year. Approximately $2,833 billion of this amount was estimated to come from new budget authority for the fiscal year, while the remainder ($970 billion) was estimated to come from budget authority enacted in prior years.

The relation of budget authority to outlays varies from program to program and depends on *spendout rates*, the rates at which funds provided by Congress are obligated and payments disbursed. In a program with a high spendout rate, most new budget authority is expended during the fiscal year; if the spendout rate is low, however, most of the outlays occur in later years. Regardless of the spendout rate, the outlays in the budget are merely estimates of the amounts that will be disbursed during the year. If payments turn out to be higher than the budget estimate, outlays will be above the budgeted level. The President and Congress control outlays indirectly by deciding on the amount of budget authority to be provided or by limiting the amount of obligations to be incurred.

Certain receipts of the federal government are accounted for as "offsets" against outlays rather than as revenues. Various fees collected by government agencies are deducted from outlays; similarly, income from the sale of certain assets are treated as *offsetting receipts*. Most such receipts are offsets against the outlays of the agencies that collect the money, but in the case of offshore oil leases and certain other activities, the revenues are deducted from the total outlays of the government.

Scope of the Budget

The budget consists of two main groups of funds: *federal funds* and *trust funds*. Federal funds—which comprise mainly the general fund—largely derive from the general exercise of the taxing power and general borrowing and for the most part are not earmarked by law to any specific program or agency. One component of federal funds, called special funds, is earmarked as to source and purpose. The use of federal funds is determined largely by appropriations acts.

Trust funds are established, under the terms of statutes that designate them as trust funds, to account for funds earmarked by specific sources and purposes. The Social Security funds are the largest of the trust funds; revenues are collected under a Social Security payroll tax and are used to pay for Social Security benefits and related purposes. The *unified budget* includes both the federal funds and the trust funds. The balances in the trust funds are borrowed by the federal government; they are counted, therefore, in the federal debt. Because these balances offset a budget deficit but are included in the federal debt, the annual increase in the debt invariably exceeds the amount of the budget deficit. For the same reason, it is possible for the federal debt to rise when the federal government has a budget surplus.

Capital and operating expenses are not segregated in the budget. Hence, monies paid for the operations of government agencies as well as for the acquisition of long-life assets (such as buildings, roads, and weapons systems) are reported as budget outlays. Proposals have been made from time to time to divide the budget into capital and operating accounts. While these proposals have not been adopted, the budget provides information showing the investment and operating outlays of the government.

The budget totals do not include all the financial transactions of the federal government. The main exclusions fall into two categories—off-budget entities and government-sponsored enterprises. In addition, the budget includes direct and guaranteed loans on the basis of the accounting rules established by the Federal Credit Reform Act of 1990, which are discussed below.

Off-budget entities are excluded by law from the budget totals. The receipts and disbursements of the Social Security trust funds (the Old-Age and Survivors Insurance Fund and the Disability Insurance Fund), as well as spending for the Postal Service Fund, are excluded from the budget totals. These transactions are shown separately in the budget. Thus, the budget now reports two deficit or surplus amounts—one excluding the Social Security trust funds and the Postal Service Fund, and the other (on a unified basis) including these entities. The latter is the main focus of discussion in both the President's budget and the congressional budget process.

The transactions of government-owned corporations (excluding the Postal Service), as well as revolving funds, are included in the budget on a net basis. That is, the amount shown in the budget is the difference between receipts and outlays, not the total activity of the enterprise or revolving fund. If, for example, a revolving fund has annual income of $150 million and disbursements of $200 million, the budget would report $50 million as net outlays.

Government-sponsored enterprises (GSEs) historically have been excluded from the budget because they were deemed to be private rather than public entities. The federal government did not own any equity in these enterprises, most of which received their financing from private sources. Although they were established by the federal government, their budgets were not reviewed by the President or Congress in the same manner as other programs. Most of these enterprises engaged in credit activities. They borrowed funds in capital markets and lent money to homeowners, farmers, and others. In total, these enterprises had assets and liabilities measured in trillions of dollars. Financial statements of the government-sponsored enterprises were published in the President's budget.

Although some GSEs continue to operate on this basis, the economic downturn and credit instability that occurred in 2008 fundamentally changed the status of two GSEs that play a significant role in the home mortgage market, Fannie Mae and Freddie Mac. In September of 2008, the Federal Housing Finance Agency (FHFA) placed the two entities in conservatorship, thereby subjecting them to control by the Federal Government until the conservatorship eventually is brought to an end.

Deficit Reduction and the Rules of Congressional Budgeting

Between the early 1980s and the late 1990s, annual consideration of the budget was dominated by concern about the budget deficit. In the mid-1980s, the deficit exceeded $150 billion and amounted to about 6% of GDP at one point. In the early 1990s, the deficit approached the $300 billion level. Following four years of surpluses (FY1998-FY2001), the budget returned to deficit for FY2002. Current budget projections show sizeable deficits persisting over the coming years.

The size of the deficit depends on how it is measured. The unified budget deficit combines all on-budget federal funds and trust funds with the off-budget entities (the Social Security trust funds and the Postal Service Fund). The unified budget deficit generally is regarded as the most comprehensive measure of the impact of the budget on the economy. A narrower measure of the deficit is derived by excluding the Social Security trust funds from the totals. This exclusion is mandated by law, although Social Security is counted in the budget in reports on the deficit. Excluding Social Security from computations of the deficit or surplus results in higher deficit or lower surplus figures.

Regardless of the measure used, it is evident that the deficit was unusually high for an extended period of time. The chronic deficits of the 1980s prompted Congress to enact the Balanced Budget and Emergency Deficit Control Act of 1985. The 1985 act established deficit targets for each year through FY1991, when the budget was to be balanced, and a sequestration process under which budgetary resources would be canceled automatically (through largely across-the-board spending cuts) if the estimated deficit exceeded the amount allowed under the act.

Even with the targets, the actual deficit for the covered years was above the targeted level. Failure to achieve the deficit targets, and other problems, led Congress to revise the process in the Budget Enforcement Act (BEA) of 1990. Sequestration procedures were retained, but the fixed deficit targets were replaced by adjustable ones (which expired at the end of FY1995), adjustable limits were imposed on discretionary spending, and a pay-as-you-go (PAYGO) process was established for revenues and direct spending. The discretionary spending limits and PAYGO process were extended (through FY1998) by the Omnibus Budget Reconciliation of 1993 and again (through FY2002) by the BEA of 1997.

Under the discretionary spending limits, different categories of discretionary spending were used for different periods. Under the 1997 changes, discretionary spending limits applied separately to defense and nondefense spending for FY1998-FY1999 and to violent crime reduction spending for FY1998-FY2000; for the remaining fiscal years, the 1997 changes merged all discretionary spending into a single, general purpose category. In 1998, as part of the Transportation Equity Act for the 21st Century, Congress added separate categories for highway and mass transit spending. Finally, in 2000, Congress added a category for conservation spending; unlike the other categories, the conservation spending category had six subcategories.

The PAYGO process under the BEA required that the budgetary impact of revenue and direct spending legislation be recorded on a multiyear "PAYGO scorecard," and that in the net any such legislation not yield a negative balance for the upcoming fiscal year. Legislation reducing revenues or increasing direct spending for a fiscal year had to be offset (in the same or other legislation) by revenue increases or reductions in direct spending for that fiscal year so that the applicable balance on the PAYGO scorecard remained at or above zero.

Under the BEA procedures, violations of the discretionary spending limits or the PAYGO requirement were to be enforced by sequestration. However, sequestration was not used for more than a decade, either because Congress and the President enacted budgetary legislation consistent with the discretionary spending limits and PAYGO requirement, or, during the latter years under the BEA, effectively waived these enforcement requirements.

The BEA enforcement procedures effectively expired toward the end of the 107th Congress. As budget deficits persisted through the last decade, proposals to restore the BEA statutory procedures had been made from time to time by members of Congress and the President, but none of the proposals were enacted until 2010. The Statutory Pay-As-You-Go Act of 2010 (P.L. 111-139) restored in statute a modified version of the PAYGO requirement for direct spending and revenue legislation.[1] Subsequently, in 2011, the Budget Control Act (P.L. 112-25) established statutory limits on discretionary spending for each year through FY2021.

Like the previous statutory PAYGO requirement under the BEA, the new statutory PAYGO requirement is intended to discourage or prevent Congress from taking certain legislative action that would increase the on-budget deficit. It generally requires that legislation affecting direct spending or revenues not increase the deficit over a six-year period and an 11-year period. Likewise, the current statutory discretionary caps established under the Budget Control Act are similar to those under the BEA. The limits essentially cap the amount of spending provided and controlled through the annual appropriations process each year, with upward adjustments to these limits permitted for certain purposes, such as for Overseas Contingency Operations.

The statutory PAYGO requirement and the statutory discretionary spending limits are enforced by sequestration—the cancellation of budgetary resources provided by laws affecting direct spending. Further information on sequestration is provided in the "The Sequestration Process" section, below.

During the 1990s to the present, the Senate has supplemented the statutory PAYGO requirement with a special PAYGO rule included in annual budget resolutions; following the expiration of the BEA procedures, the Senate extended its PAYGO rule (currently through FY2017). The Senate PAYGO rule currently prohibits the consideration of any legislation that proposes changes in direct spending or revenue that increase the deficit over six-year and 11-year time periods (including the current fiscal year). The House adopted its own PAYGO rule for the first time at the beginning of the 110th Congress. At the beginning of the 112th Congress, however, the House modified this rule, renaming it CutGo, or cut-as-you-go, to prohibit the consideration of any legislation that would have the net effect of increasing direct spending over the same two time periods.

Budgeting for Discretionary and Direct Spending

The distinction drawn by the BEA and the congressional budget process between discretionary spending (which is controlled through the annual appropriations process) and direct spending (which is provided outside of the annual appropriations process) recognized that the federal government has somewhat different, though overlapping, means of dealing with these two types of spending. One set of procedures pertained to discretionary spending, another to direct spending.

Most of the direct spending subject to the PAYGO process under the BEA involved entitlement programs; the rest consisted of other forms of mandatory spending provided through authorizing legislation and interest payments. In fact, entitlements now account for about half of total federal spending (all direct spending, including net interest, accounts for about 60% of the total). The impressive feature of this trend is that most of the growth in spending and in the number of recipients has been built into existing law; for the most part, it has not been the result of new legislation.

---

[1] For more detailed information on the statutory PAYGO requirement, see CRS Report R41157, *The Statutory Pay-As-You-Go Act of 2010: Summary and Legislative History*, by Bill Heniff Jr.

The procedures for discretionary and direct spending converge at two critical points in federal budgeting: formulation of the President's budget and formulation of the congressional budget resolution. Both of these policy statements encompass discretionary and direct spending, but the procedures used in budgeting for these types of expenditure differ greatly. The distinctions have some notable exceptions. Some procedures associated with direct spending are applied to particular types of discretionary programs, and vice versa. Nevertheless, the generalizations presented here help to explain the complications of the budget process and explain how decisions are made.

(1) Budgetary Impact of Authorizing Legislation. An authorization for a discretionary spending program is only a license to enact an appropriation. The amount of budgetary resources available for spending is determined in annual appropriations acts. For direct spending programs (principally entitlements), on the other hand, the authorizing legislation either provides, or effectively mandates the appropriation of, budget authority. In those entitlement programs that are subject to annual appropriation, the Appropriations Committees have little or no discretion as to the amounts they provide.

(2) Committees That Provide or Mandate Budget Authority. The Appropriations Committees have jurisdiction and effective control over discretionary spending programs, while authorizing committees effectively control direct spending programs (including those funded in annual appropriations acts). In fact, committee jurisdiction determines whether a program is classified as discretionary or direct spending. All spending under the effective control of the Appropriations Committees is discretionary; everything else is direct spending. Accordingly, when legislation establishes a program as discretionary or direct spending, it not only determines the character of spending but the locus of congressional committee control as well.

(3) Frequency of Decision-Making. Discretionary appropriations are, with few exceptions, made annually for the current or next fiscal year. Direct spending programs typically are established in permanent law that continues in effect until such time as it is revised or terminated by another law. The fact that many entitlements have annual appropriations does not diminish the permanence of the laws governing the amounts spent. It should be noted, however, that some direct spending programs, such as Medicare, have been subject to frequent legislative changes. The purpose of such legislation has been to modify existing law, not to provide annual funding.

(4) Means of Enforcing the Budget Resolution. The procedures used by Congress to enforce the policies set forth in the annual budget resolution differ somewhat for discretionary and direct spending programs. For both types of spending, Congress relies on allocations made under Section 302 of the 1974 Congressional Budget Act to ensure that spending legislation reported by House and Senate committees conforms to established budget policies. But although this procedure is effective in controlling new legislation—both annual appropriations measures and new entitlement legislation—it is not an effective control on the spending that results from existing laws. Hence, Congress relies on reconciliation procedures to enforce budget policies with respect to existing spending and revenue laws. Reconciliation is not currently applied to discretionary programs funded in annual appropriations measures.

(5) Statutory Controls. Discretionary programs have been subject to the spending limits set in the BEA. Direct spending has not been capped, but has operated under the PAYGO process, which required that direct spending and revenue legislation enacted for a fiscal year not cause the deficit to rise or the surplus to decrease. The lack of caps was due to the fact that most direct spending

programs are open-ended, with spending determined by eligibility rules and payment formulas in existing law rather than by new legislation.

Budget enforcement depends on timely information concerning the status of federal revenues and spending. When it acts on legislation, Congress must be informed of the estimated impact on future budgets. Measuring these impacts often is referred to as "scoring" or "scorekeeping." Scoring discretionary spending measures is a much simpler task than scoring direct spending and revenue legislation. In the latter case, scoring always is done in reference to baseline projections of future revenues and spending.

Most appropriations are for a definite amount and the budget authority is provided for a single fiscal year. The main task is to estimate the outlays that will derive in the next year and beyond from the budget authority provided in the appropriations bill. CBO and the Appropriations Committees base these estimates on outlay (or spendout) rates—the percentage of budget authority that is spent in each year. These outlay rates vary by account and are based on historical records. For example, if $1 billion is appropriated to an account which has a spendout rate of 80% in the first fiscal year that funds become available, the outlay estimate for that fiscal year will be $800 million; the remaining $200 million will become outlays in one or more subsequent years.

Scorekeeping is much more complex in enforcing budget rules, such as the PAYGO requirements, relating to direct spending and revenues. For one thing, unlike appropriations, revenue and direct spending legislation usually is open-ended; it does not specify the amount by which revenue or spending will be changed. For another, the impact of this type of legislation continues in future years. In enforcing the PAYGO requirements, Congress had to estimate the revenue gain or loss for the ensuing five years under the BEA, and for 11 years under the more recent statutory and Senate PAYGO rules. Congress cannot develop the revenue estimates simply by referring to the text of the legislation being scored. It must also take into account the behavior of taxpayers, economic conditions, and other factors that affect revenue collection.

Congress scores revenue and direct spending legislation by reference to baseline projections issued by CBO, sometimes in cooperation with OMB. The baseline is an extrapolation of future budget conditions, typically for each of the next five years, based on the assumption that current policies will continue in effect. The baseline projections incorporate assumptions about future inflation and workload changes mandated by law. These projections are made for the budget aggregates as well as for individual programs and accounts.

When Congress considers revenue or direct spending legislation, CBO estimates the amount of revenues or outlays that would ensue if the measure were enacted; in the case of most revenue legislation, CBO uses estimates prepared by the Joint Tax Committee. It then compares this amount with the baseline projection to score the legislation. Thus, the score measures budgetary impact as the difference between the amount projected under current policies and the amount estimated if the legislation were enacted. A score is reported for each of the years and often for the sum of the years as well.

Congress usually relies on the CBO score while it is considering legislation. The BEA gave OMB the authority to determine whether offsets or a sequester were required under the PAYGO rules. The more recent Statutory Pay-As-You-Go Act of 2010 provides that the budgetary effects of individual direct spending and revenue legislation are to be determined either by a reference in the legislation to a statement of budgetary effects submitted for printing in the *Congressional Record* by the chair of the House or Senate Budget Committee prior to passage, or by OMB if no appropriate reference in the legislation or statement exists. The OMB and CBO scores on legislation sometimes differ.

In addition to enforcing PAYGO, baseline projections and scoring are used in computing the amount of deficit reduction agreed to in budget summit negotiations between the President and Congress and enacted in reconciliation acts.

Budgeting for Direct and Guaranteed Loans

The Federal Credit Reform Act of 1990 made fundamental changes in the budgetary treatment of direct loans and guaranteed loans. The reform, which first became effective for FY1992, shifted the accounting basis for federally provided or guaranteed credit from the amount of cash flowing into or out of the Treasury to the estimated subsidy cost of the loans. Credit reform entails complex procedures for estimating these subsidy costs and new accounting mechanisms for recording various loan transactions. The changes have had only a modest impact on budget totals but a substantial impact on budgeting for particular loan programs.

The new system requires that budget authority and outlays be budgeted for the estimated subsidy cost of direct and guaranteed loans. This cost is defined in the 1990 act as "the estimated long-term cost to the Government of a direct loan or a loan guarantee, calculated on a net present value basis, excluding administrative costs."

Under the new system, Congress appropriates budget authority or provides indefinite authority equal to the subsidy cost. This budget authority is placed in a program account from which funds are disbursed to a financing account.

The Budget Cycle

Federal budgeting is a cyclical activity that begins with the formulation of the President's annual budget and concludes with the audit and review of expenditures. The process spreads over a multi-year period. The main stages are formulation of the President's budget, congressional budget actions, implementation of the budget, and audit and review. While the basic steps continue from year to year, particular procedures often vary in accord with the style of the President, the economic and political considerations under which the budget is prepared and implemented, and other factors.

The activities related to a single fiscal year usually stretch over a period of two-and-a-half calendar years (or longer). As the budget is being considered, federal agencies must deal with three different fiscal years at the same time: implementing the budget for the current fiscal year; seeking funds from Congress for the next fiscal year; and planning for the fiscal year after that.

The Presidential Budget Process

The President's budget, officially referred to as the *Budget of the United States Government*, is required by law to be submitted to Congress early in the legislative session, no later than the first Monday in February. The budget consists of estimates of spending, revenues, borrowing, and debt; policy and legislative recommendations; detailed estimates of the financial operations of federal agencies and programs; data on the actual and projected performance of the economy; and other information supporting the President's recommendations.

The President's budget is only a request to Congress; Congress is not required to adopt his recommendations. Nevertheless, the power to formulate and submit the budget is a vital tool in the President's direction of the executive branch and of national policy. The President's proposals often influence congressional revenue and spending decisions, though the extent of the influence varies from year to year and depends more on political and fiscal conditions than on the legal status of the budget.

The Constitution does not provide for a budget, nor does it require the President to make recommendations concerning the revenues and spending of the federal government. Until 1921, the federal government operated without a comprehensive presidential budget process. The Budget and Accounting Act of 1921, as amended, provides for a national budget system. Its basic requirement is that the President should prepare and submit a budget to Congress each year. The 1921 act established the Bureau of the Budget, now named the Office of Management and Budget (OMB), to assist the President in preparing and implementing the executive budget. Although it has been amended many times, this statute provides the legal basis for the presidential budget, prescribes much of its content, and defines the roles of the President and the agencies in the process.

Formulation and Content of the President's Budget

Preparation of the President's budget typically begins in the spring (or earlier) each year, at least nine months before the budget is submitted to Congress, about 17 months before the start of the fiscal year to which it pertains, and about 29 months before the close of that fiscal year. The early stages of budget preparation occur in federal agencies. When they begin work on the budget for a fiscal year, agencies already are implementing the budget for the fiscal year in progress and awaiting final appropriations actions and other legislative decisions for the fiscal year after that. The long lead times and the fact that appropriations have not yet been made for the next year mean that the budget is prepared with a great deal of uncertainty about economic conditions, presidential policies, and congressional actions.

As agencies formulate their budgets, they maintain continuing contact with the OMB examiners assigned to them. These contacts provide agencies with guidance in preparing their budgets and also enable them to alert OMB to any needs or problems that may loom ahead. Agency requests are submitted to OMB in late summer or early fall; these are reviewed by OMB staff in consultation with the President and his aides. The 1921 Budget and Accounting Act bars agencies from submitting their budget requests directly to Congress. Moreover, OMB regulations provide for confidentiality in all budget requests and recommendations prior to the transmittal of the President's budget to Congress. However, it is quite common for internal budget documents to become public while the budget is still being formulated.

The format and content of the budget are partly determined by law, but the 1921 act authorizes the President to set forth the budget "in such form and detail" as he may determine. Over the years, there has been an increase in the types of information and explanatory material presented in the budget documents.

In most years, the budget is submitted as a multi-volume set consisting of a main document setting forth the President's message to Congress and an analysis and justification of his major proposals (the *Budget*) and supplementary documents providing account and program level details, historical information, and special budgetary analyses (the *Budget Appendix*, *Historical Tables*, and *Analytical Perspectives*), among other things.

Much of the budget is an estimate of requirements under existing law rather than a request for congressional action (more than half of the budget authority in the budget becomes available without congressional action). The President is required to submit a budget update (reflecting changed economic conditions, congressional actions, and other factors), referred to as the *Mid-Session Review*, by July 15 each year. The President may revise his recommendations any time during the year.

Executive Interaction with Congress

The President and his budget office have an important role once the budget is submitted to Congress. OMB officials and other presidential advisors appear before congressional committees to discuss overall policy and economic issues, but they generally leave formal discussions of specific programs to the affected agencies. Agencies thus bear the principal responsibility for defending the President's program recommendations at congressional hearings.

Agencies are supposed to justify the President's recommendations, not their own. OMB maintains an elaborate legislative clearance process to ensure that agency budget justifications, testimony, and other submissions are consistent with presidential policy. As the session unfolds, the President may formally signal his position on pending legislation through the issuance of a Statement of Administration Policy (SAP). These statements, which are maintained by OMB on its website, are sometimes used to convey a veto threat against legislation the President feels requires modifications to meet his approval.

Increasingly in recent years, the President and his chief budgetary aides have engaged in extensive negotiations with Congress over major budgetary legislation. These negotiations sometimes have occurred as formal budget "summits" and at other times as less visible, behind-the-scenes activities.

The Congressional Budget Process

The Congressional Budget and Impoundment Control Act of 1974 establishes the congressional budget process as the means by which Congress coordinates the various budget-related actions (such as the consideration of appropriations and revenue measures) taken by it during the course of the year. The process is centered around an annual concurrent resolution on the budget that sets aggregate budget policies and functional priorities for at least the next five fiscal years.

Because a concurrent resolution is not a law—it cannot be signed or vetoed by the President—the budget resolution does not have statutory effect; no money can be raised or spent pursuant to it. The main purpose of the budget resolution is to establish the framework within which Congress considers separate revenue, spending, and other budget-related legislation. Revenue and spending amounts set in the budget resolution establish the basis for the enforcement of congressional budget policies through points of order. The budget resolution also initiates the reconciliation process for conforming existing revenue and spending laws to congressional budget policies.

Formulation and Content of the Budget Resolution

The congressional budget process begins upon the presentation of the President's budget in January or February (see **Table 1**). The timetable set forth in the 1974 Congressional Budget Act calls for the final adoption of the budget resolution by April 15, well before the beginning of the new fiscal year on October 1. Although the House and Senate often pass the budget resolution separately before April 15, they often do not reach final agreement on it until after the deadline— sometimes months later. The 1974 act bars consideration of revenue, spending, and debt-limit measures for the upcoming fiscal year until the budget resolution for that year has been adopted, but certain exceptions are provided (such as the exception that allows the House to consider the regular appropriations bills after May 15, even if the budget resolution has not been adopted by then).

Table 1. Congressional Budget Process Timetable

Deadline	Action to be completed
First Monday in February	President submits budget to Congress.
February 15	CBO submits report on economic and budget outlook to Budget committees.
Six weeks after President's budget is submitted	Committees submit reports on views and estimates to respective Budget Committee.
April 1	Senate Budget Committee reports budget resolution.
April 15	Congress completes action on budget resolution.
June 10	House Appropriations Committee reports last regular appropriations bill.
June 30	House completes action on regular appropriations bills and any required reconciliation legislation.
July 15	President submits mid-session review of his budget to Congress.
October 1	Fiscal year begins.

Source: Compiled by the Congressional Research Service.

The 1974 Congressional Budget Act requires the budget resolution, for each fiscal year covered, to set forth budget aggregates and spending levels for each functional category of the budget. The aggregates included in the budget resolution are as follows:

- total revenues (and the amount by which the total is to be changed by legislative action);
- total new budget authority and outlays;
- the surplus or deficit; and
- the debt limit.

With regard to each of the functional categories, the budget resolution must indicate for each fiscal year the amounts of new budget authority and outlays, and they must add up to the corresponding spending or aggregates.

Aggregate amounts in the budget resolution do not reflect the revenues or spending of the Social Security trust funds, although these amounts are set forth separately in the budget resolution for purposes of Senate enforcement procedures.

The budget resolution does not allocate funds among specific programs or accounts, but the major program assumptions underlying the functional amounts are often discussed in the reports accompanying each resolution. Some recent reports have contained detailed information on the program levels assumed in the resolution. These assumptions are not binding on the affected committees. Finally, the 1974 act allows certain additional matters to be included in the budget resolution. The most important optional feature of a budget resolution is reconciliation directives (discussed below).

The House and Senate Budget Committees are responsible for marking up and reporting the budget resolution. In the course of developing the budget resolution, the Budget Committees hold hearings, receive "views and estimates" reports from other committees, and obtain information from CBO. These "views and estimates" reports of House and Senate committees provide the Budget Committees with information on the preferences and legislative plans of congressional committees regarding budgetary matters within their jurisdiction.

CBO assists the Budget Committees in developing the budget resolution by issuing, early each year, a report on the economic and budget outlook that includes baseline budget projections. The baseline projections presented in the report are supported by more detailed projections for accounts and programs; CBO usually revises the baseline projections one or more times before the Budget Committees mark up the budget resolution. In addition, CBO issues a report analyzing the President's budgetary proposals in light of CBO's own economic and technical assumptions. In past years, CBO also issued an annual report on spending and revenue options for reducing the deficit or maintaining the surplus.

The extent to which the Budget Committees (and the House and Senate) consider particular programs when they act on the budget resolution varies from year to year. Specific program decisions are supposed to be left to the Appropriations Committees and other committees of jurisdiction, but there is a strong likelihood that major issues will be discussed in markup, in the Budget Committees' reports, and during floor consideration of the budget resolution. Although any programmatic assumptions generated in this process are not binding on the committees of jurisdiction, they often influence the final outcome.

Floor consideration of the budget resolution is guided by House and Senate rules and practices. In the House, the Rules Committee usually reports a *special rule* (a simple House resolution), which, once approved, establishes the terms and conditions under which the budget resolution is considered. This special rule typically specifies which amendments may be considered and the sequence in which they are to be offered and voted on. It has been the practice in recent years to allow consideration of a few amendments (as substitutes for the entire resolution) that present broad policy choices. In the Senate, the amendment process is less structured, relying on agreements reached by the leadership through a broad consultative process. The amendments offered in the Senate may entail major policy choices or may be focused on a single issue.

Achievement of the policies set forth in the annual budget resolution depends on the legislative actions taken by Congress (and their approval or disapproval by the President), the performance of the economy, and technical considerations. Many of the factors that determine whether budgetary goals will be met are beyond the direct control of Congress. If economic conditions—

growth, employment levels, inflation, and so forth—vary significantly from projected levels, so too will actual levels of revenue and spending. Similarly, actual levels may differ substantially if the technical factors upon which estimates are based, such as the rate at which agencies spend their discretionary funds or participants become eligible for entitlement programs, prove faulty.

Budget Resolution Enforcement

Congress's regular tools for enforcing the budget resolution each year are overall spending ceilings and revenue floors and committee allocations and subdivisions of spending. In addition, the Senate in some years has enforced discretionary spending limits in the budget resolution, which paralleled the adjustable limits established in statute and enforced by the sequestration process, and both chambers have imposed additional rules on direct spending and revenue legislation. Finally, the House and Senate in recent years have included procedural features in budget resolutions to limit the use of advance appropriations.

In order for the enforcement procedures to work, Congress must have access to complete and up-to-date budgetary information so that it can relate individual measures to overall budget policies and determine whether adoption of a particular measure would be consistent with those policies. Substantive and procedural points of order are designed to obtain congressional compliance with budget rules. A point of order may bar House or Senate consideration of legislation that violates the spending ceilings and revenue floors in the budget resolution, committee subdivisions of spending, or congressional budget procedures.

Budget Resolution Aggregates

In the early years after the 1974 Congressional Budget Act, the principal enforcement mechanism was the ceiling on total budget authority and outlays and the floor under total revenues set forth in the budget resolution. The limitations inherent in this mechanism soon became apparent. For example, the issue of controlling breaches of the spending ceilings usually did not arise until Congress acted on supplemental appropriations acts, when the fiscal year was well underway. The emergency nature of the legislation often made it difficult to uphold the ceilings.

Changes sometimes are made in budget resolutions by virtue of the operation of reserve funds. Generally, reserve funds allow increases to be made in various spending levels associated with the budget resolution for legislation meeting criteria specified in the budget resolution, as long as any increases spending from the legislation is offset (e.g., by revenue increases) so as to be deficit neutral.

Allocations of Spending to Committees

In view of the inadequacies in the early years of congressional budgeting of relying on enforcement of the budget totals, Congress changed the focus of enforcement in the 1980s to the committee allocations and subdivisions of spending made pursuant to Section 302 of the act. The key to enforcing budget policy is to relate the budgetary impact of individual pieces of legislation to the overall budget policy. Because Congress operates through its committee system, an essential step in linking particular measures to the budget is to allocate the spending amounts set forth in the budget resolution among House and Senate committees.

Section 302(a) provides for allocations to committees to be made in the statement of managers accompanying the conference report on the budget resolution. A Section 302(a) allocation is made to each committee which has jurisdiction over spending, both for the budget year and the full period covered by the budget resolution—at least five fiscal years.

The committee allocations do not take into account jurisdiction over discretionary authorizations funded in annual appropriations acts. The amounts of new budget authority and outlays allocated to committees in the House or Senate may not exceed the aggregate amounts of budget authority and outlays set forth in the budget resolution. Although these allocations are made by the Budget Committees, they are not the unilateral preferences of these committees. They are based on assumptions and understandings developed in the course of formulating the budget resolution.

After the allocations are made under Section 302(a), the House and Senate Appropriations Committees subdivide the amounts they receive among their 12 subcommittees, as required by Section 302(b). The subcommittees' Section 302(b) subdivisions may not exceed the total amount allocated to the committee. Each Appropriations Committee reports its subdivisions to its respective chamber; the appropriations bills may not be considered until such a report has been filed.

Scoring and Cost Estimates

As mentioned previously, scoring (also called scorekeeping) is the process of measuring the budgetary effects of pending and enacted legislation and assessing its impact on a budget plan—in this case, the budget resolution. In the congressional budget process, scoring serves several broad purposes. First, scoring informs members of Congress and the public about the budgetary consequences of their actions. When a budgetary measure is under consideration, scoring information lets members know whether adopting the amendment or passing the bill at hand would breach the budget. Further, scoring information enables members to judge what must be done in upcoming legislative action to achieve the year's budgetary goals. Finally, scoring is designed to assist Congress in enforcing its budget plans. In this regard, scorekeeping is used largely to determine whether points of order under the 1974 act may be sustained against legislation violating budget resolution levels.

The principal scorekeepers for Congress are the House and Senate Budget Committees, which provide the presiding officers of their respective chambers with the estimates needed to determine if legislation violates the aggregate levels in the budget resolution or the committee subdivisions of spending. The Budget Committees make summary scoring reports available to members on a frequent basis, usually geared to the pace of legislative activity. CBO assists Congress in these activities by preparing cost estimates of legislation, which are included in committee reports, and scoring reports for the Budget committees. The Joint Committee on Taxation supports Congress by preparing estimates of the budgetary impact of revenue legislation.

Points of Order

The 1974 Congressional Budget Act provides for both substantive and procedural points of order to block violations of budget resolution policies and congressional budget procedures. One element of substantive enforcement is based on Section 311 of the act, which bars Congress from considering legislation that would cause total revenues to fall below the level set in the budget resolution or total new budget authority or total outlays to exceed the budgeted level. The House and Senate both enforce the spending ceilings for the first fiscal year only; the revenue floor, however, is enforced for the first fiscal year and the full number of fiscal years covered by the budget resolution.

In the House (but not the Senate), Section 311 does not apply to spending legislation if the committee reporting the measure has stayed within its allocation of new discretionary budget authority. Accordingly, the House may take up any spending measure that is within the appropriate committee allocations, even if it would cause total spending to be exceeded. Neither chamber bars spending legislation that would cause functional allocations in the budget resolution to be exceeded.

Section 302(f) of the 1974 act bars the House and Senate from considering any spending measure that would cause the relevant committee's spending allocations to be exceeded; in the House, the point of order applies only to violations of allocations of new discretionary budget authority. Further, the point of order also applies to suballocations of spending made by the Appropriations Committees.

In addition to points of order to enforce compliance with the budget resolution and the allocations and subdivisions made pursuant to it, the 1974 act contains points of order to ensure compliance with its procedures. Perhaps the most important of these is Section 303, which bars consideration of any revenue, spending, entitlement, or debt-limit measure prior to adoption of the budget resolution. However, the rules of the House permit it to consider regular appropriations bills after May 15, even if the budget resolution has not yet been adopted.

When the House or Senate considers a revenue or a spending measure, the chairman of the respective Budget Committee sometimes makes a statement advising the chamber as to whether the measure violates any of these points of order. If no point of order is made, or if the point of order is waived, the House or Senate may consider a measure despite any violations of the 1974 act. The House often waives points of order by adopting a special rule. The Senate may waive points of order by unanimous consent or by motion under Section 904 of the act. The Senate requires a three-fifths vote of the membership to waive certain provisions of the act.

In several past years, the House and Senate failed to reach agreement on a budget resolution. On these occasions, one or both houses agreed to their own "deeming resolutions," which established the basis for enforcing points of order under the 1974 act in that house only.

The Sequestration Process

Sequestration was the principle means used to enforce statutory budget enforcement policies in place from 1985 through 2002, and it is the principle means used to enforce the PAYGO requirement under the Statutory Pay-As-You-Go Act of 2010 and the statutory limits on discretionary spending under the Budget Control Act of 2011 (BCA). In addition, sequestration is used to achieve a portion of the spending reductions required as a result of the failure to enact deficit reduction legislation tied to the Joint Committee on Deficit Reduction, as provided by the BCA.[2]

---

[2] For further information on the BCA, see CRS Report R41965, *The Budget Control Act of 2011*, by Bill Heniff Jr., Elizabeth Rybicki, and Shannon M. Mahan.

Sequestration involves the issuance of a presidential order that permanently cancels budgetary resources (except for revolving funds, special funds, trust funds, and certain offsetting collections) for the purpose of achieving a required amount of outlay savings to reduce the deficit. Once sequestration is triggered by an executive determination, spending reductions are made automatically; this process, therefore, is regarded by many as providing a strong incentive for Congress and the President to reach agreement on legislation that would avoid a sequester.

From its inception in 1985 until its revision by the Budget Enforcement Act (BEA) in 1990, the process was tied solely to the enforcement of fixed deficit targets. The BEA changed the sequestration process substantially. First, it effectively eliminated the deficit targets as a factor in budget enforcement. Second, the BEA established adjustable limits on discretionary spending funded in the annual appropriations process. Third, the BEA created pay-as-you-go procedures to require that increases in direct spending (i.e., spending controlled outside of the annual appropriations process) or decreases in revenues due to legislative action were offset so that there was effectively no net increase in the deficit or reduction of the surplus.

The BEA established adjustable limits on discretionary spending for FY1991-FY1995. These limits were extended through FY1998 in 1993. The Budget Enforcement Act (BEA) of 1997 revised the limits for FY1998 and provided new limits through FY2002. The limits were established for the following categories of discretionary spending: defense and nondefense, for FY1998-FY1999; discretionary (a single, general purpose category), for FY2000-FY2002; and violent crime reduction, for FY1998-FY2000. In 1998, as part of the Transportation Equity Act for the 21st Century, separate categories were added for highway and mass transit spending. Finally, a spending conservation category was added in 2000. The limits expired at the end of FY2002. As noted above, the Budget Control Act of 2011 revived the statutory limits on discretionary spending by establishing them for each year through FY2021.

The original discretionary spending limits had to be adjusted periodically by the President for various factors, including (among others), changes in concepts and definitions, a special outlay allowance (to accommodate estimating differences between OMB and CBO), and the enactment of legislation providing emergency funding and funding for the International Monetary Fund, international arrearages, an earned income tax credit compliance initiative, and other specially designated purposes. The more recent limits, under the BCA, may be adjusted for spending designated for emergencies, Overseas Contingency Operations, and disaster relief, among other specified purposes.

Under the pay-as-you-go (PAYGO) process created by the BEA, legislation increasing direct spending or decreasing revenues for a fiscal year had to be offset so that the balance on the PAYGO scorecard for that year did not fall below zero. The PAYGO process did not require any offsetting action when the spending increase or revenue decrease was due to the operation of existing law, such as an increase in the number of persons participating in the Medicare program. Direct spending consists largely of spending for entitlement programs. Most direct spending and revenue programs are established under permanent law, so there is not necessarily any need for recurring legislative action on them (and the PAYGO process did not require such action).

The PAYGO process did not preclude Congress from enacting legislation to increase direct spending; it only required that the increase be offset by reductions in other direct spending programs (which could include increases in offsetting receipts), by increases in revenues, or by a combination of the two in order to avoid a sequester. If a sequester under this process was required, it would have had to offset the amount of any net deficit increase (or surplus reduction) for the fiscal year caused by the enactment of legislation in the current and prior sessions of Congress, and would have been applied to nonexempt direct spending programs.

Spending for Social Security benefits and federal deposit insurance commitments, as well as emergency direct spending and revenue legislation (so designated by both the President and by Congress), was exempted completely from the PAYGO sequestration process. All remaining direct spending programs were covered by the PAYGO process to the extent that legislation affecting their spending levels was counted in determining whether a net increase or decrease in the deficit has occurred for a fiscal year. If a PAYGO sequester had occurred, however, many direct spending programs would have been exempt from reduction.

In 1997, coverage of the PAYGO requirement was extended to legislation enacted through FY2002; however, the PAYGO process was slated to remain in effect through FY2006 to deal with the outyear effects of such measures. Consequently, a PAYGO sequester could have occurred in FY2003-FY2006 based on legislation enacted before the end of FY2002. At the end of the 107th Congress, legislation was enacted setting all of the remaining PAYGO balances to zero, effectively terminating the PAYGO requirement under the BEA.

The multiple sequestration procedures established by the BEA remained automatic, to be triggered by a report from the OMB director. For sequestration purposes generally, there was only one triggering report issued each year (just after the end of the congressional session), but preliminary and update sequestration reports were issued earlier in the session. Additionally, OMB reports triggering a sequester for discretionary spending could be issued during the following session if legislative developments so warranted (i.e., the enactment of supplemental appropriations). The CBO director was required to provide advisory sequestration reports, shortly before the OMB director's reports were due.

Sequestration procedures could be suspended in the event a declaration of war was enacted or if Congress enacted a special joint resolution triggered by the issuance of a CBO report indicating "low growth" in the economy. Also, there were several special procedures under the act by which the final sequestration order for a fiscal year could be modified or the implementation of the order affected.

As noted above, sequestration has been revived to enforce more recent statutory budget enforcement rules. First, the Statutory Pay-As-You-Go Act of 2010, enacted on February 12, 2010, restored the sequestration process to enforce the new PAYGO requirement for direct spending and revenue legislation. Generally, the new statutory PAYGO process provides that if the net effect of direct spending and revenue legislation enacted during a year increases the deficit, budgetary resources in certain direct spending programs are cut in order to eliminate the increase in the deficit. Specifically, the average budgetary effects (i.e., any increase or decrease in the deficit) over five- and 10-year periods[3] of each direct spending and revenue act are placed on five- and 10-year scorecards, respectively. Like the PAYGO process under the BEA, the sequestration process is triggered by a report from the OMB director issued 14 days after Congress adjourns at the end of a session. If either scorecard shows a positive balance (referred to as a debit) for the budget year, the President is required to issue a sequestration order cancelling

---

[3] The five-year period covers the budget year and four fiscal years thereafter, and the 10-year period covers the budget year and nine fiscal years thereafter. The statutory rule also requires that any budgetary effects for the current year must be added to the budgetary effects for the budget year.

budgetary resources in non-exempt direct spending programs sufficient to eliminate the balance (the larger balance if both scorecards show a positive balance).[4]

Second, the Budget Control Act of 2011 restored the sequestration process, including the reports and triggering mechanisms under the earlier BEA, to enforce the recently established statutory limits on discretionary spending for each fiscal year through FY2021. In addition, the BCA uses sequestration to achieve additional deficit reduction. Specifically, the BCA created a Joint Select Committee on Deficit Reduction, composed of an equal number of Senators and Members of the House, and instructed it to develop a proposal that would reduce the deficit by at least $1.5 trillion over the FY2012-FY2021 period. In the event that this Joint Committee was not successful, the BCA established the automatic process to reduce spending (a fallback mechanism to automatically reduce spending), beginning in 2013. If legislation developed by the Joint Committee did not reduce the deficit by at least $1.2 trillion through FY2021 and was not enacted by January 15, 2012, this automatic process would be triggered. The process presumably was intended to encourage agreement on such deficit reduction, either by enacting the Joint Committee proposal or possibly by enacting other legislation (through existing congressional procedures) prior to the beginning of 2013, when the automatic process would begin to make reductions. Given that the Joint Committee was not successful, this automatic process has been triggered. Therefore, at the time of this writing, spending reductions are scheduled to be made on January 2, 2013, with a sequester of $109 billion in budgetary resources equally divided between defense and nondefense spending, unless Congress and the President agree by statute to repeal or modify the automatic process. Additional spending reductions are also scheduled to be achieved in direct spending in each year through FY2021.

Spending Legislation

The spending policies of the budget resolution generally are implemented through two different types of spending legislation. Policies involving discretionary spending are implemented in the context of annual appropriations acts, whereas policies affecting direct or mandatory spending (which, for the most part, involves entitlement programs) are carried out in substantive legislation.

All discretionary spending is under the jurisdiction of the House and Senate Appropriations Committees. Direct spending is under the jurisdiction of the various legislative committees of the House and Senate; the House Ways and Means Committee and the Senate Finance Committee have the largest shares of direct spending jurisdiction. (Some entitlement programs, such as Medicaid, are funded in annual appropriations acts, but such spending is not considered to be discretionary.) The enforcement procedures under the congressional budget process, mentioned above, apply equally to discretionary and direct spending.

---

[4] Most direct spending programs and activities, including Social Security benefits, veterans' programs, retirement and disability benefits, and low-income programs, among others, are exempt from any sequestration. In addition, the amount of any sequestration is limited to 4% for Medicare and 2% for certain health and medical care activities.

Authorizing Measures

The rules of the House and (to a lesser extent) the Senate require that agencies and programs be authorized in law before an appropriation is made for them. An authorizing act is a law that (1) establishes a program or agency and the terms and conditions under which it operates; and (2) authorizes the enactment of appropriations for that program or agency. Authorizing legislation may originate in either the House or the Senate and may be considered any time during the year. Many agencies and programs have temporary authorizations that have to be renewed annually or every few years.

Action on appropriations measures sometimes is delayed by the failure of Congress to enact necessary authorizing legislation. The House and Senate often waive or disregard their rules against unauthorized appropriations for ongoing programs that have not yet been reauthorized.

The budgetary impact of authorizing legislation depends on whether it contains only discretionary authorizations (for which funding is provided in annual appropriations acts) or direct spending, which itself enables an agency to enter into obligations.

The Annual Appropriations Process

An appropriations act is a law passed by Congress that provides federal agencies legal authority to incur obligations and the Treasury Department authority to make payments for designated purposes. The power of appropriation derives from the Constitution, which in Article I, Section 9, provides that "[n]o money shall be drawn from the Treasury but in consequence of appropriations made by law." The power to appropriate is exclusively a legislative power; it functions as a limitation on the executive branch. An agency may not spend more than the amount appropriated to it, and it may use available funds only for the purposes and according to the conditions provided by Congress.

The Constitution does not require annual appropriations, but since the First Congress the practice has been to make appropriations for a single fiscal year. Appropriations must be used (obligated) in the fiscal year for which they are provided, unless the law provides that they shall be available for a longer period of time. All provisions in an appropriations act, such as limitations on the use of funds, expire at the end of the fiscal year, unless the language of the act extends their period of effectiveness.

The President requests annual appropriations in his budget submitted each year. In support of the President's appropriations requests, agencies submit justification materials to the House and Senate Appropriations Committees. These materials provide considerably more detail than is contained in the President's budget and are used in support of agency testimony during Appropriations subcommittee hearings on the President's budget.

Congress passes three main types of appropriations measures. *Regular appropriations* acts provide budget authority to agencies for the next fiscal year. *Supplemental appropriations* acts provide additional budget authority during the current fiscal year when the regular appropriation is insufficient or to finance activities not provided for in the regular appropriation. *Continuing appropriations* acts provide stop-gap (or full-year) funding for agencies that have not received a regular appropriation.

In a typical session, Congress acts on 12 regular appropriations bills and at least two supplemental appropriations measures. Because of recurring delays in the appropriations process, Congress also typically passes one or more continuing appropriations each year. The scope and duration of these measures depend on the status of the regular appropriations bills and the degree of budgetary conflict between the President and Congress. In recent years, Congress has merged two or more of the regular appropriations acts for a fiscal year into a single, omnibus appropriations act.

By precedent, appropriations originate in the House of Representatives. In the House, appropriations measures are originated by the Appropriations Committee (when it marks up or reports the measure) rather than being introduced by a member beforehand. Before the full Committee acts on the bill, it is considered in the relevant Appropriations subcommittee (the House and Senate Appropriations Committees have 12 parallel subcommittees). The House subcommittees typically hold extensive hearings on appropriations requests shortly after the President's budget is submitted. In marking up their appropriations bills, the various subcommittees are guided by the discretionary spending limits and the allocations made to them under Section 302 of the 1974 Congressional Budget Act.

The Senate usually considers appropriations measures after they have been passed by the House. When House action on appropriations bills is delayed, however, the Senate sometimes expedites its actions by considering a Senate-numbered bill up to the stage of final passage. Upon receipt of the House-passed bill in the Senate, it is amended with the text that the Senate already has agreed to (as a single amendment) and then passed by the Senate. Hearings in the Senate Appropriations subcommittees generally are not as extensive as those held by counterpart subcommittees in the House.

The basic unit of an appropriation is an account. A single unnumbered paragraph in an appropriations act comprises one account and all provisions of that paragraph pertain to that account and to no other, unless the text expressly gives them broader scope. Any provision limiting the use of funds enacted in that paragraph is a restriction on that account alone.

Over the years, appropriations have been consolidated into a relatively small number of accounts. It is typical for a federal agency to have a single account for all its expenses of operation and additional accounts for other purposes such as construction. Accordingly, most appropriation accounts encompass a number of activities or projects. The appropriation sometimes earmarks specific amounts to particular activities within the account, but the more common practice is to provide detailed information on the amounts intended for each activity in other sources (principally, the committee reports accompanying the measures).

In addition to the substantive limitations (and other provisions) associated with each account, each appropriations act has "general provisions" that apply to all of the accounts in a title or in the whole act. These general provisions appear as numbered sections, usually at the end of the title or the act.

The standard appropriation is for a single fiscal year—the funds have to be obligated during the fiscal year for which they are provided; they lapse if not obligated by the end of that year. An appropriation that does not mention the period during which the funds are to be available is a one-year appropriation. Congress also makes no-year appropriations by specifying that the funds shall remain available until expended. No-year funds are carried over to future years, even if they have not been obligated. Congress sometimes makes multiyear appropriations, which provide for funds to be available for two or more fiscal years.

Appropriations measures also contain other types of provisions that serve specialized purposes. These include provisions that liquidate (pay off) obligations made pursuant to certain contract authority; reappropriate funds provided in previous years; transfer funds from one account to another; rescind funds (or release deferred funds); or set ceilings on the amount of obligations that can be made under permanent appropriations, on the amount of direct or guaranteed loans that can be made, or on the amount of administrative expenses that can be incurred during the fiscal year. In addition to providing funds, appropriations acts often contain substantive limitations on government agencies.

Detailed information on how funds are to be spent, along with other directives or guidance, is provided in the reports accompanying the various appropriations measures. Agencies ordinarily abide by report language in spending the funds appropriated by Congress.

The appropriations reports do not comment on every item of expenditure. Report language is most likely when the Appropriations Committee prefers to spend more or less on a particular item than the President has requested or when the committee wants to earmark funds for a particular project or activity. When a particular item is mentioned by the committee, there is a strong expectation that the agency will adhere to the instructions.

Revenue Legislation

Article I, Section 8 of the Constitution gives Congress the power to levy "taxes, duties, imposts, and excises." Section 7 of this article requires that all revenue measures originate in the House of Representatives.

In the House, revenue legislation is under the jurisdiction of the Ways and Means Committee; in the Senate, jurisdiction is held by the Finance Committee. While House rules bar other committees from reporting revenue legislation, sometimes another committee will report legislation levying user fees on a class that benefits from a particular service or program or that is being regulated by a federal agency. In many of these cases, the user fee legislation is referred subsequently to the Ways and Means Committee.

Most revenues derive from existing provisions of the tax code or Social Security law, which continue in effect from year to year unless changed by Congress. This tax structure can be expected to produce increasing amounts of revenue in future years as the economy expands and incomes rise. Nevertheless, Congress usually makes some changes in the tax laws each year, either to raise or lower revenues or to redistribute the tax burden.

Congress typically acts on revenue legislation pursuant to proposals in the President's budget. An early step in congressional work on revenue legislation is publication by CBO of its own estimates (developed in consultation with the Joint Tax Committee) of the revenue impact of the President's budget proposals. The congressional estimates often differ significantly from those presented in the President's budget.

The revenue totals in the budget resolution establish the framework for subsequent action on revenue measures. The budget resolution contains only revenue totals and total recommended changes; it does not allocate these totals among revenue sources (although it does set out Medicare receipts separately), nor does it specify which provisions of the tax code are to be changed.

The House and Senate often consider major revenue measures, such as the Tax Reform Act of 1986, under their regular legislative procedures. However, as has been the case with direct spending programs, many of the most significant changes in revenue policy in recent years have been made in the context of the reconciliation process. Although revenue changes are usually incorporated into omnibus budget reconciliation measures, along with spending changes (and sometimes debt-limit increases), revenue reconciliation legislation may be considered on a separate legislative track (e.g., the Tax Equity and Fiscal Responsibility Act of 1982).

When the reconciliation process is used to advance revenue reductions (or spending increases) that would lead to a deficit, or would enlarge an existing deficit, Section 313 of the 1974 Congressional Budget Act (referred to as the Senate's "Byrd rule") limits the legislative changes to the period covered by the reconciliation directives. Accordingly, some recent tax cuts have been subject to sunset dates.

In enacting revenue legislation, Congress often establishes or alters tax expenditures. The term "tax expenditures" is defined in the 1974 Congressional Budget Act to include revenue losses due to deductions, exemptions, credits, and other exceptions to the basic tax structure. Tax expenditures are a means by which the federal government pursues public policy objectives and can be regarded as alternatives to other policy instruments such as grants or loans. The Joint Tax Committee estimates the revenue effects of legislation changing tax expenditures, and it also publishes five-year projections of these provisions as an annual committee print.

Debt-Limit Legislation

When the revenues collected by the federal government are not sufficient to cover its expenditures, it must finance the shortfall through borrowing. Federal borrowing is subject to a public debt limit established by statute. When the federal government operates with a budget deficit, the public debt limit must be increased periodically. The frequency of congressional action to raise the debt limit has ranged in the past from several times in one year to once in several years. When the federal government incurred large and growing surpluses in recent years, Congress did not have to increase the debt limit, but the enactment of increases in the debt limit has again become necessary with the recurrence of deficits.

Legislation to raise the public debt limit falls under the jurisdiction of the House Ways and Means Committee and the Senate Finance Committee. Although consideration of such measures in the House usually is constrained through the use of special rules, Senate action sometimes is far-ranging with regard to the issues covered. In the past, the Senate has added many non-germane provisions to debt-limit measures, such as the 1985 Balanced Budget Act.

In 1979, the House amended its rules to provide for the automatic engrossment of a measure increasing the debt limit upon final adoption of the conference report on the budget resolution. The rule, House Rule XLIX (commonly referred to as the Gephardt rule), was intended to facilitate quick action on debt increases. However, the Senate had no comparable rule. For years, the House and Senate could enact debt-limit legislation originating under the Gephardt rule or arising under conventional legislative procedures. During the past decade, Congress has enacted debt-limit increases as part of omnibus budget reconciliation measures, continuing appropriations acts, and other legislation. The House recodified the Gephardt rule as House Rule XXIII at the beginning of the 106th Congress, repealed it at the beginning of the 107th Congress, and reinstated it, as new Rule XXVII, at the beginning of the 108th Congress. At the beginning of the 112th Congress, the House once again repealed the rule, thereby requiring the House to vote directly on any legislation that changes the statutory limit on the public debt.

Reconciliation Legislation

Beginning in 1980, Congress has used reconciliation legislation to implement many of its most significant budget policies. Section 310 of the 1974 Congressional Budget Act sets forth a special procedure for the development and consideration of reconciliation legislation. Reconciliation legislation is used by Congress to bring existing revenue and spending law into conformity with the policies in the budget resolution. Reconciliation is an optional process, but Congress has used it more years than not; during the period covering 1980 through 2010, 20 reconciliation measures were enacted into law and three were vetoed.

The reconciliation process has two stages—the adoption of reconciliation instructions in the budget resolution and the enactment of reconciliation legislation that implements changes in revenue or spending laws. Although reconciliation has been used since 1980, specific procedures tend to vary from year to year.

Reconciliation is used to change the amount of revenues, budget authority, or outlays generated by existing law. In a few instances, reconciliation has been used to adjust the public debt limit. On the spending side, the process focuses on entitlement laws; it may not be used, however, to impel changes in Social Security law. Reconciliation sometimes has been applied to discretionary authorizations (which are funded in annual appropriations acts), but this is not the usual practice.

Reconciliation was used in the 1980s and into the 1990s as a deficit-reduction tool. Beginning in the latter part of the 1990s, some reconciliation measures were used principally to reduce revenues, thereby increasing the deficit. At the beginning of the 110th Congress, both chambers adopted rules requiring that reconciliation be used solely for deficit reduction.

Reconciliation Directives

Reconciliation begins with a directive in a budget resolution instructing designated committees to report legislation changing existing law or pending legislation. These instructions have three components: (1) they name the committee (or committees) that are directed to report legislation; (2) they specify the amounts by which existing laws are to be changed (but do not identify how these changes are to be made, which laws are to be altered, or the programs to be affected); and (3) they usually set a deadline by which the designated committees are to recommend the changes in law. The instructions typically cover the same fiscal years covered by the budget resolution. Sometimes, budget resolutions have provided for more than one reconciliation measure to be considered during a session.

The dollar amounts are computed with reference to the CBO baseline. Thus, a change represents the amount by which revenues or spending would decrease or increase from baseline levels as a result of changes made in existing law. This computation is itself based on assumptions about the future level of revenues or spending under current law (or policy) and about the dollar changes that would ensue from new legislation. Hence, the savings associated with the reconciliation process are assumed savings. The actual changes in revenues or spending may differ from those estimated when the reconciliation instructions are formulated.

Although the instructions do not mention the programs to be changed, they are based on assumptions as to the savings or deficit reduction (or, in some cases, increases) that would result from particular changes in revenue provisions or spending programs. These program assumptions are sometimes printed in the reports on the budget resolution. Even when the assumptions are not published, committees and members usually have a good idea of the specific program changes contemplated by the reconciliation instructions.

A committee has discretion to decide on the legislative changes to be recommended. It is not bound by the program changes recommended or assumed by the Budget Committees in the reports accompanying the budget resolution. Further, a committee has to recommend legislation estimated to produce dollar changes for each category delineated in the instructions to it.

When a budget resolution containing a reconciliation instruction has been approved by Congress, the instruction has the status of an order by the House and Senate to designated committees to recommend legislation, usually by a date certain. It is expected that committees will carry out the instructions of their parent chamber, but the 1974 Congressional Budget Act does not provide any sanctions against committees that fail to do so.

Development and Consideration of Reconciliation Measures

When more than one committee in the House and Senate is subject to reconciliation directives, the proposed legislative changes usually are consolidated by the Budget Committees into an omnibus bill. The 1974 Congressional Budget Act does not permit the Budget Committees to revise substantively the legislation recommended by the committees of jurisdiction. This restriction pertains even when the Budget Committees estimate that the proposed legislation will fall short of the dollar changes called for in the instructions. Sometimes, the Budget Committees, working with the leadership, develop alternatives to the committee recommendations, to be offered as floor amendments, so as to achieve greater compliance with the reconciliation directives.

The 1974 act requires that amendments offered to reconciliation legislation in either the House or the Senate be deficit neutral. To meet this requirement, an amendment reducing revenues or increasing spending must offset these deficit increases by equivalent revenue increases or spending cuts.

During the first several years' experience with reconciliation, the legislation contained many provisions that were extraneous to the purpose of reducing the deficit. The reconciliation submissions of committees included such things as provisions that had no budgetary effect, that increased spending or reduced revenues, or that violated another committee's jurisdiction.

In 1985, the Senate adopted a rule (commonly referred to as the Byrd rule) on a temporary basis as a means of curbing these practices. The Byrd rule has been extended and modified several times over the years. In 1990, the Byrd rule was incorporated into the 1974 Congressional Budget Act as Section 313 and made permanent.

Although the House has no rule comparable to the Senate's Byrd rule, it may use other devices to control the inclusion of extraneous matter in reconciliation legislation. In particular, the House may use special rules to make in order amendments that strike such matter.

House and Senate Earmark Disclosure Rules

In 2007, both the House and Senate adopted rules intended to bring more transparency to the process surrounding earmarks. Although the definitions vary, an earmark generally is considered to be an allocation of resources to specifically targeted beneficiaries, either through discretionary or direct spending, limited tax benefits, or limited tariff benefits.[5]

Concern about earmarking practices arose over such provisions being inserted into legislation or accompanying reports without any identification of the sponsor, and the belief that many earmarks were not subject to proper scrutiny and diverted resources to lesser-priority items or items without sufficient justification, thereby contributing to wasteful spending or revenue loss.

In response to this concern, earmark rules were adopted that vary by chamber, but include three main features. The first feature is a requirement that members requesting a congressional earmark provide a written statement to the chair and ranking minority member of the committee of jurisdiction that includes the member's name, the name and address of the intended earmark recipient, the purpose of the earmark, and a certification that the member or member's spouse has no financial interest in such an earmark. (The Senate rule applies not only to the spouse but the entire immediate family.)

The second feature is a general requirement that committees provide a list of all earmarks included in reported legislation. The third feature is a point of order against legislation that is not accompanied by a list of included earmarks. These vary by chamber.

House of Representatives

House Rule XXI, clause 9, generally requires that certain types of measures be accompanied by a list of earmarks or a statement that the measure contains no earmarks.[6] If the list of earmarks or the statement that no earmark exists in the measure is absent, a point of order may lie against the measure's floor consideration. The point of order applies to the absence of such a list or statement, and does not speak to the completeness or the accuracy of such document.

House earmark disclosure rules apply to any congressional earmark included in either the text of the measure or the committee report accompanying the measure, as well as the conference report and joint explanatory statement. The disclosure requirements apply to items in authorizing, appropriations, and revenue legislation. Furthermore, they apply not only to measures reported by committees, but also to unreported measures, "manager's amendments," Senate measures, and conference reports.

---

[5] For more information on House and Senate earmark rules, see CRS Report RL34462, *House and Senate Procedural Rules Concerning Earmark Disclosure*, by Sandy Streeter.

[6] Depending upon the type of measure, the list or statement is to be included either in the measure's accompanying report, or printed in the *Congressional Record*.

These earmark disclosure requirements, however, do not apply to all legislation at all times. Not subject to the rule are floor amendments (except a "manager's amendment"), amendments between the Houses, or amendments considered as adopted under a self-executing special rule, including a committee amendment in the nature of a substitute made in order as original text. The earmark rule, as with most House rules, is not self enforcing and relies instead on a member raising a point of order if the rule is violated. When a measure is considered under suspension of the rules, House rules are laid aside and earmark disclosure rules are, therefore, waived. It is not in order to consider a special rule that waives earmark requirements under the House rule.

The Senate

Senate Rule XLIV creates a point of order against a motion to proceed to consider a measure or a vote on adoption of a conference report, unless the chair of the committee or the Majority Leader (or designee) certifies that a complete list of earmarks and the name of each Senator requesting each earmark is available on a publicly accessible congressional website in a searchable form at least 48 hours before the vote. If a Senator proposes a floor amendment containing an earmark, those items must be printed in the *Congressional Record* as soon as "practicable."[7] If the earmark certification requirements have not been met, a point of order may lie against consideration of the measure or a vote on the conference report. The point of order applies only to the absence of such certification, and does not speak to its accuracy.

Senate earmark disclosure rules apply to any congressional earmark included in either the text of the bill or a committee report accompanying the bill, as well as a conference report and joint explanatory statement. The disclosure requirements apply to items in authorizing, appropriations, and revenue legislation. Furthermore, they apply not only to measures reported by committees, but also to unreported measures, amendments, House bills, and conference reports.

The earmark rule may be waived either by unanimous consent or by motion, which requires the affirmative vote of three-fifths of all Senators (60, if there are no vacancies).[8] The earmark rule, as with most Senate rules, is not self enforcing and relies instead on a Senator raising a point of order if the rule is violated.

While not embodied in either chamber's rules, an earmark "ban" or "moratorium" is currently in effect in both the House and Senate, enforced by committee and chamber leadership.[9]

---

[7] The rule does not apply to all earmarks in floor amendments, only those "not included in the bill or joint resolution as placed on the calendar or as reported by any committee, in a committee report on such a bill or joint resolution, or a committee report of the Senate on a companion measure," as stated in Rule XLIV, paragraph 4(a).

[8] These points of order may also be waived if the Majority and Minority Leaders jointly agree that "such a waiver is necessary as a result of a significant disruption to Senate facilities or to the availability of the Internet." Senate Rule XLIV, paragraph 12.

[9] The House Republican Conference Rules include a standing order, adopted December 8, 2010, stating that "It is the policy of the House Republican Conference that no Member shall request a congressional earmark, limited tax benefit, or limited tariff benefit, as such terms have been described in the Rules of the House," available at http://www.gop.gov/about/rules?standing-orders-for-the-112th. In the Senate, the chair of the Committee on Appropriations announced in a press release on February 1, 2011, and again on February 2, 2012, that an earmark moratorium would be enforced on all FY2011, FY2012, and FY2013 appropriations bills, available at http://www.appropriations.senate.gov/news.cfm?method=news.view&id=188dc791-4b0d-459e-b8d9-4ede5ca299e7 and http://www.appropriations.senate.gov/news.cfm?method=news.view&id=3883059e-7a0c-496e-8d51-440aa7c2d57c.

Impoundment and Line-Item Veto

Impoundment

Although an appropriation limits the amounts that can be spent, it also establishes the expectation that the available funds will be used to carry out authorized activities. Therefore, when an agency fails to use all or part of an appropriation, it deviates from the intentions of Congress. The Impoundment Control Act of 1974 prescribes rules and procedures for instances in which available funds are impounded.

An impoundment is an action or inaction by the President or a federal agency that delays or withholds the obligation or expenditure of budget authority provided in law. The 1974 Impoundment Control Act divides impoundments into two categories and establishes distinct procedures for each. A *deferral* delays the use of funds; a *rescission* is a presidential request that Congress rescind (cancel) an appropriation or other form of budget authority. Deferral and rescission are exclusive and comprehensive categories; an impoundment is either a rescission or a deferral—it cannot be both or something else.

Although impoundments are defined broadly by the 1974 act, in practice they are limited to major actions that affect the level or rate of expenditure. As a general practice, only deliberate curtailments of expenditure are reported as impoundments; actions having other purposes that incidently affect the rate of spending are not recorded as impoundments. For example, if an agency were to delay the award of a contract because of a dispute with a vendor, the delay would not be an impoundment; if the delay were for the purpose of reducing an expenditure, it would be an impoundment. The line between routine administrative actions and impoundments is not clear and controversy occasionally arises as to whether a particular action constitutes an impoundment.

Rescissions

To propose a rescission, the President must submit a message to Congress specifying the amount to be rescinded, the accounts and programs involved, the estimated fiscal and program effects, and the reasons for the rescission. Multiple rescissions can be grouped in a single message. After the message has been submitted to it, Congress has 45 days of "continuous session" (usually a larger number of calendar days) during which it can pass a rescission bill. Congress may rescind all, part, or none of the amount proposed by the President.

If Congress does not approve a rescission in legislation by the expiration of this period, the President must make the funds available for obligation and expenditure. If the President fails to release funds at the expiration of the 45-day period for proposed rescissions, the comptroller general may bring suit to compel their release. This has been a rare occurrence, however.

Deferrals

To defer funds, the President submits a message to Congress setting forth the amount, the affected account and program, the reasons for the deferral, the estimated fiscal and program effects, and the period of time during which the funds are to be deferred. The President may not propose a deferral for a period of time beyond the end of the fiscal year, nor may he propose a deferral that would cause the funds to lapse or otherwise prevent an agency from spending appropriated funds prudently. In accounts where unobligated funds remain available beyond the fiscal year, the President may defer the funds again in the next fiscal year.

At present, the President may defer only for the reasons set forth in the Antideficiency Act, including to provide for contingencies, to achieve savings made possible by or through changes in requirements or greater efficiency of operations, and as specifically provided by law. He may not defer funds for policy reasons (e.g., to curtail overall federal spending or because he is opposed to a particular program).

The comptroller general reviews all proposed rescissions and deferrals and advises Congress of their legality and possible budgetary and program effects. The comptroller general also notifies Congress of any rescission or deferral not reported by the President and may reclassify an improperly classified impoundment. In all cases, a notification to Congress by the comptroller general has the same legal effect as an impoundment message of the President.

The 1974 Impoundment Control Act provides for special types of legislation—rescission bills and deferral resolutions—for Congress to use in exercising its impoundment control powers. However, pursuant to court decisions that held the legislative veto to be unconstitutional, Congress may not use deferral resolutions to disapprove a deferral. Further, Congress has been reluctant to use rescission bills regularly. Congress, instead, usually acts on impoundment matters within the framework of the annual appropriations measures.

Line-Item Veto

During the 104th Congress, the Line Item Veto Act (P.L. 104-130) was enacted as an amendment to the 1974 Impoundment Control Act. The Supreme Court ruled the Line Item Veto Act unconstitutional in June 1998.

The authority granted to the President under the Line Item Veto Act differed markedly from the veto authority available to most chief executives at the state level. First, the President could not veto individual parts of legislation submitted for his approval. Under normal constitutional procedures, the President must approve or veto any measure in its entirety. His authority to use the line-item veto came into play only after a measure had been signed into law. Second, this authority applied not only to annual appropriations, but extended to new entitlement spending and targeted tax benefits as well. The line-item veto authority was intended to be in effect for eight years, from the beginning of 1997 through the end of 2004.

The Line Item Veto Act reversed the presumption underlying the process for the consideration of rescissions under the 1974 Impoundment Control Act. Under the Line Item Veto Act, presidential proposals would take effect unless overturned by legislative action. The act authorized the President to identify at enactment individual items in legislation that he proposed not go into effect. The identification was based not just upon the statutory language, but on the entire legislative history and documentation. The President had to notify Congress promptly of his proposals and provide supporting information. Congress had to respond within a limited period of time by enacting a law if it wanted to disapprove the President's proposals; otherwise, they would take effect permanently.

President Clinton exercised the line-item veto authority several times during the 1997 session before the act was declared unconstitutional.

Author Contact Information

Bill Heniff Jr., Coordinator
Analyst on Congress and the Legislative Process
wheniff@crs.loc.gov, 7-8646

Jessica Tollestrup
Analyst on Congress and the Legislative Process
jtollestrup@crs.loc.gov, 7-0941

Megan Suzanne Lynch
Analyst on Congress and the Legislative Process
mlynch@crs.loc.gov, 7-7853

Acknowledgments

This report was originally written by Robert Keith, formerly a Specialist in American National Government at CRS, and Allen Schick, formerly a Consultant at CRS. The analysts listed on the cover of this report, and under the "author contact information," updated portions of the report and are available to answer questions related to the federal budget process.